Yayoi Kusama

From Here to Infinity

Sarah Suzuki

**Illustrated by
Ellen Weinstein**

With reproductions of works
by Yayoi Kusama

The Museum of Modern Art
New York

Yayoi Kusama was born in the country of Japan, on the island of Honshu, in a town called Matsumoto City. An old palace made of wood and stone overlooked a moat where swans swam; the streets were lined with little shops; and snow-capped mountains rose in the distance, swallowing up the sun as it went down in the evening.

Yayoi's family owned nurseries where all kinds of flowers and vegetables grew, and workers tended the plants as they matured from seeds to sprouts to stalks.

But Yayoi yearned for a different life, far from the countryside. She dreamed about what lay beyond the mountains, in places far from Matsumoto City. She longed to leave home and see the world.

Yayoi's mother wanted her to stay home and learn old-fashioned manners—how to dress elegantly, walk demurely, eat politely—and find a proper husband.

But Yayoi wanted to be an artist. Every day she went outside with ink and brushes and paper. She drew things she saw and things she imagined. She looked closely at the pebbles that lined the riverbed and at the leaves and stalks of plants, and she drew them as chains of tiny cells that looked like dots.

When she was older and studying in art school, her teachers disapproved of her work, and they demanded that Yayoi paint in the traditional, precise Japanese style.

She wanted to go where she could live without rules.

When she was twenty-eight years old she packed up her silk kimonos and thousands of drawings and stuffed dollar bills into the toes of her shoes.

It was her first airplane trip. There were only four other passengers, and the weather was stormy, with rain and lightning. The airplane wobbled and dipped as it flew to America.

In New York, Yayoi went to the top of the Empire State Building, the tallest building in a city full of tall buildings. When she looked down, she saw buses and cars and yellow taxis zooming up and down the avenues, and bankers and teachers and artists rushing to work: from up on the eighty-sixth floor they looked like dots.

She felt very far from quiet Matsumoto City and her mother's rules. Here, it seemed, anything was possible.

Yayoi set about turning her drawings of dots into paintings. The dollar bills that she had brought to America quickly ran out, and she spent what little money she had left on paints and canvases. She worked day and night. She painted when she was cold, she painted when she was hungry, she painted when she was lonely. And she turned her dots into sculptures, too, into soft stuffed tubes that covered sofas and chairs and boats.

She was devoted to her dots—for her they were a way of thinking about the world among the stars, as one dot among millions of others. They were a way of thinking about infinity.

Sometimes, when she grew frustrated, she visited The Museum of Modern Art. She gazed at paintings by other artists, and she thought about why and how they were made. She looked at pictures of dancing girls and swirling night skies, trying to solve them as if they were puzzles.

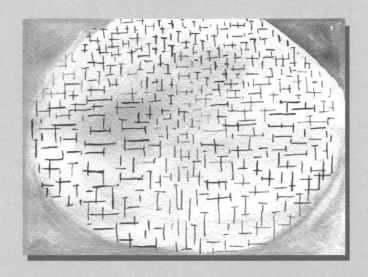

Her paintings seemed so different from those she had seen at MoMA. When she at last was ready to show her work in public, she invited all the friends she had made in New York. When she arrived at the gallery, a crowd was spilling out onto the sidewalk. Her friends lifted her into the air, shouting,

"Yayoi, you've finally done it!"

Word about her artwork spread quickly. Her friends told their friends, newspapers wrote about her work, and reporters clamored to interview her about her dots. Now she began to show them in other cities all over the United States and Europe.

NEWS STAND

KUSAMA

Visual

KUNST

Kusama!

Gallery

AR

Art W

Her dots were covering the world.

They appeared in Venice in thousands of dot-shaped mirrors scattered over a big green lawn . . .

. . . on a pumpkin on a pier . . .

. . . on dresses and T-shirts, on people walking down the street . . .

. . . and in mirrored rooms where glowing dots were reflected and reflected again. An infinity of dots!

Having visited many countries all over the world, Yayoi returned to Japan. The country had changed since she left, with many different artists challenging the old traditional style, as Yayoi had been doing all along.

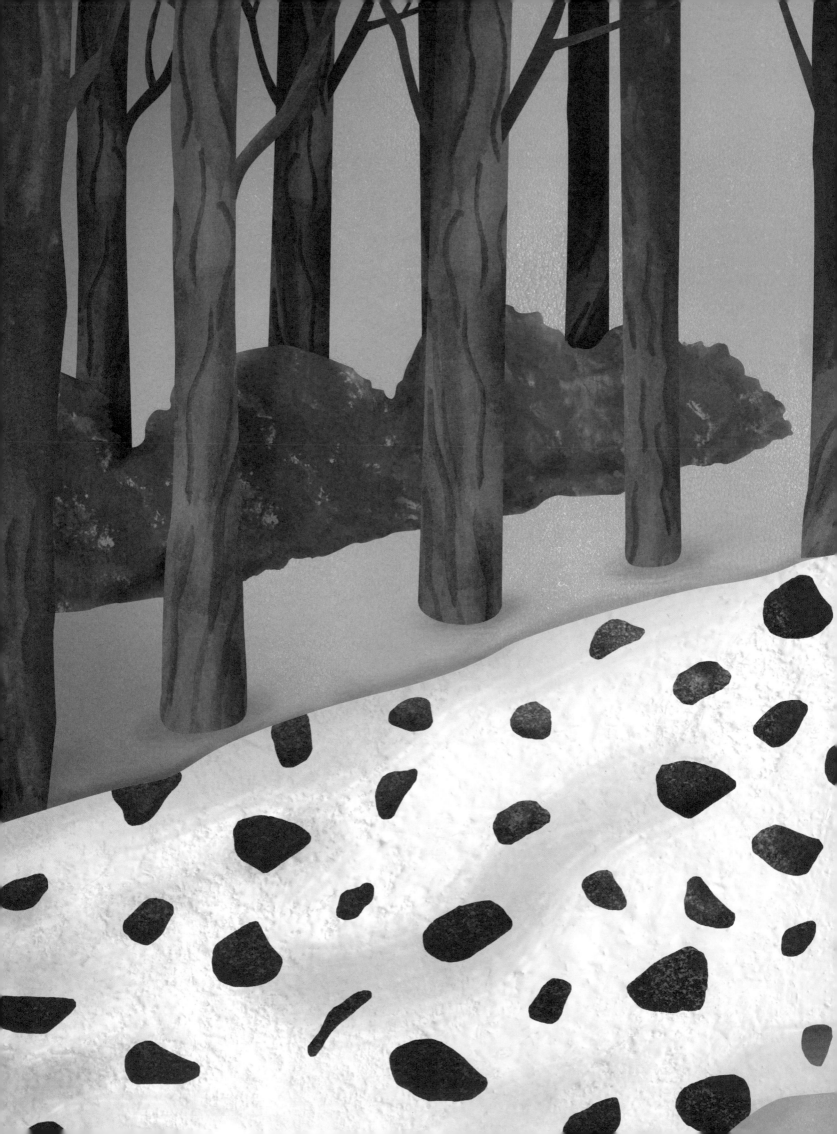

She still lives in Japan, and she continues to paint her dots every day.

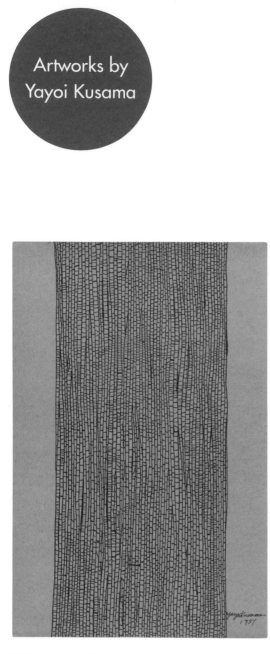

Infinity Nets. 1951

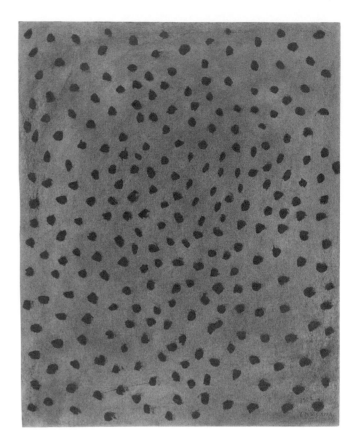

Untitled. 1952

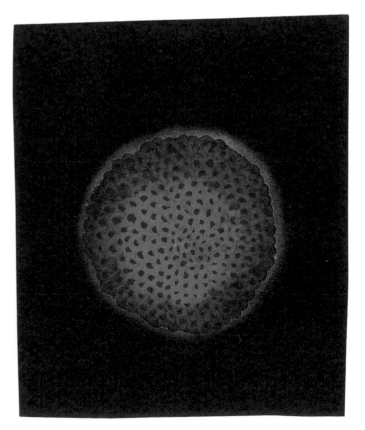

Flower. 1953 and (1963)

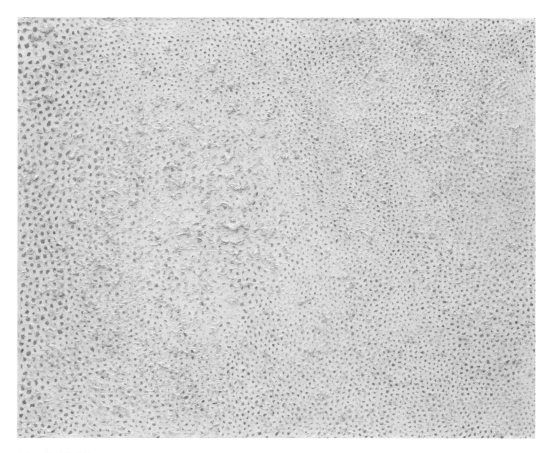

No. F. 1959

Accumulation No. 1. 1962

INFINITY MIRRORED
ROOM—THE SOULS
OF MILLIONS OF LIGHT
YEARS AWAY. 2013

The obliteration room.
2002–present

The artist Yayoi Kusama was born in Matsumoto, Japan, in 1929. For more than sixty years she has made many different types of art, including drawings, paintings, photographs, and installation and performance works. Although scholars and critics have connected her to various styles, including Pop art and Minimalism, she has always thought of herself as distinct from these movements. Kusama's work is deeply influenced by the dreams and visions she had as a child, in which the world was covered in polka dots, and she has covered her paintings, drawings, and sculptures with layers of dots, nets, squiggles, and stickers. She is widely considered to be the most popular artist in the world.

Kusama, now eighty-eight years old, still goes to her studio and makes art every day. Millions of people all over the world, in North and South America, Europe, and Asia, visit her exhibitions and share photos of her works on the Internet. The collection of The Museum of Modern Art, New York, includes examples of the artist's work in different mediums, spanning the course of her career from the 1950s to the present.

Works by Yayoi Kusama shown on pages 28–29:

Infinity Nets. 1951. Ink on paper, 15 ½ x 10 ⅛ in. (39.4 x 25.7 cm). The Museum of Modern Art, New York. Purchased with funds provided by Jo Carole and Ronald S. Lauder

Untitled. 1952. Ink on paper. 15 ¾ x 11 ⅞ in. (40 x 30 cm). The Museum of Modern Art, New York. Purchase

Flower. 1953 and (1963). Ink, gouache, and pastel on paper, 15 ¾ x 13 ¼ in. (40.1 x 33.8 cm). The Museum of Modern Art, New York. Purchased with funds given by Sheldon H. Solow

No. F. 1959. Oil on canvas, 41 ½ x 52 in. (105.4 x 132.1 cm). The Museum of Modern Art, New York. Sid R. Bass Fund

Accumulation No. 1. 1962. Sewn stuffed fabric, paint, and chair fringe, 37 x 39 x 43 in. (94 x 99.1 x 109.2 cm). The Museum of Modern Art, New York.Gift of William B. Jaffe and Evelyn A. J. Hall (by exchange)

INFINITY MIRRORED ROOM—THE SOULS OF MILLIONS OF LIGHT YEARS AWAY. 2013. Wood, metal, glass mirrors, plastic, acrylic panel, rubber, LED lighting system, acrylic balls, and water, 9 ft. 5 ¼ in. x 13 ft. 7 ½ in. x 13 ft. 7 ½ in. (287.7 x 415.3 x 415.3 cm).

The obliteration room. 2002–present. Furniture, white paint, and dot stickers, dimensions variable. Collaboration between Yayoi Kusama and Queensland Art Gallery, Australia. Commissioned by Queensland Art Gallery. Gift of the artist through the Queensland Art Gallery Foundation, 2012. Queensland Art Gallery Collection

Works shown on pages 14–15, from left to right:

Vincent van Gogh (Dutch, 1853–1890). *The Starry Night*. Saint Rémy, June 1889. Oil on canvas, 29 x 36 ¼ in. (73.7 x 92.1 cm). The Museum of Modern Art, New York. Acquired through the Lillie P. Bliss Bequest

René Magritte (Belgian, 1898–1967). *The False Mirror*. Le Perreux-sur-Marne, 1928. Oil on canvas, 21 ¼ x 31 ⅞ in. (54 x 80.9 cm). The Museum of Modern Art, New York. Purchase

Henri Matisse (French, 1869–1954). *Dance (I)*. Paris, Boulevard des Invalides, early 1909. Oil on canvas, 8 ft. 6 ½ in. x 12 ft. 9 ½ in. (259.7 x 390.1 cm). The Museum of Modern Art, New York. Gift of Nelson A. Rockefeller in honor of Alfred H. Barr, Jr.

Henri Rousseau (French, 1844–1910). *The Sleeping Gypsy*. 1897. Oil on canvas, 51 in. x 6 ft. 7 in. (129.5 x 200.7 cm). The Museum of Modern Art, New York. Gift of Mrs. Simon Guggenheim

Piet Mondrian (Dutch, 1872–1944). *Pier and Ocean 5 (Sea and Starry Sky)*. (1915) (inscribed 1914). Charcoal and watercolor on paper, 34 ⅝ x 44 in. (87.9 x 111.7 cm). The Museum of Modern Art, New York. Mrs. Simon Guggenheim Fund

Produced by the Department of Publications
The Museum of Modern Art, New York

Christopher Hudson, Publisher
Chul R. Kim, Associate Publisher
Don McMahon, Editorial Director
Marc Sapir, Production Director

Edited by Chul R. Kim and Emily Hall
Designed by Naomi Mizusaki, Supermarket
Production by Hannah Kim
Printed and bound by Ofset Yapimevi, Istanbul

With special thanks to Ms. Yayoi Kusama for letting us tell her story.

Thanks also to Rebecca Ashby-Colón, Carol Coffin, Cari Frisch, Laura Hoptman, Julia Joern, Elizabeth Margulies, Chris Rawson, Eriko Takeuchi, Ann Temkin, Amanda Washburn, and Wendy Woon

Support for this publication was provided by The International Council of The Museum of Modern Art.

This book is typeset in Futura.
The paper is 150 gsm Amber Graphic.

© 2017 The Museum of Modern Art, New York
Second printing 2018
Third printing 2019
Fourth printing 2020
Fifth printing 2022
Illustrations © 2017 Ellen Weinstein
All works by Yayoi Kusama © 2017 Yayoi Kusama

All rights reserved

Library of Congress Control Number: 2017944524
ISBN: 978-1-63345-039-4

Published by The Museum of Modern Art
11 West 53 Street
New York, New York 10019
www.moma.org

Distributed in the United States and Canada by Abrams Books for Young Readers, an imprint of ABRAMS, New York

Distributed outside the United States and Canada by Thames & Hudson Ltd., London

Printed in Turkey

Photograph Credits: Courtesy David Zwirner, New York; Ota Fine Arts, Tokyo/Singapore; Victoria Miro, London; YAYOI KUSAMA Inc.: *The obliteration room; INFINITY MIRRORED ROOM—THE SOULS OF MILLIONS LIGHT YEARS AWAY;* photograph of the artist

Queensland Art Gallery/Gallery of Modern Art, photograph by Mark Sherwood: *The obliteration room*

The Museum of Modern Art, New York, Department of Imaging Services; photograph by Thomas Griesel: *Dance (I), The Sleeping Gypsy;* photograph by Paige Knight: *Flower;* photograph by Jonathan Muzikar: *No. F, Pier and Ocean 5 (Sea and Starry Sky);* photograph by John Wronn: *Infinity Nets, Untitled, Accumulation No. 1, The Starry Night, The False Mirror*